Sources and credits

Barry Ulanov's A Handbook of Jazz (New York: Viking, 1959)
http://www.plosin.com/beatbegins/archive/Ulanov.htm

Glossary of jazz and popular music, from Wikipedia, the free encyclopedia (text available under the Creative Commons Attribution-ShareAlike License)
https://en.wikipedia.org/wiki/Glossary_of_jazz_and_popular_music

Virginia Tech Multimedia Music Dictionary
https://web.archive.org/web/20141022022300/http://www.music.vt.edu/musicdictionary/

Jazz in America Glossary by The Thelonious Monk Institute of Jazz with courtesy of Thelonious Monk Institute of Jazz.
http://www.jazzinamerica.org/jazzresources/glossary/a/i

Interpretations of Jazz Band Literature – Musical terms used in jazz. U.S. Army Music Master Classes
http://www.music.army.mil/education/

Jazz Glossary: the language of Jazz music
Copyright © 1998-2017 A Passion for Jazz, with courtesy of A Passion for Jazz!
https://www.apassion4jazz.net/glossary.html

Nicholas Brunner : A Glossary of Jazz Terms
http://nicholas_bruner.tripod.com/id3.html

Kuumbwa Jazz Jazz Glossary
https://www.kuumbwajazz.org/wp-content/uploads/2015/03/edu-jazz-report-glossary.pdf

Quizlet Jazz Glossary
https://quizlet.com/131656005/jazz-glossary-flash-cards/

Jazz Glossary - Columbia Center for Teaching and Learning (text available under a Creative Commons Attribution-Noncommercial-Share Alike 3.0 Unported License).
http://ccnmtl.columbia.edu/projects/jazzglossary/

Jazz St. Louis Glossary
http://www.jazzstl.org/education-outreach/elementary-curriculum-partnerships/jazz-concepts-for-the-young-beginner/glossary-of-terms/

Jazz dance termonology by Phyllis Eckler
http://faculty.lacitycollege.edu/ecklerp/Jazz_Dance_terminology.htm

Jazz Slang Dictionary
http://www.the-jazz-cat.com/jazz-slang-dictionary.html

Norton & Company Jazz glossary :
http://www.wwnorton.com/college/music/jazz/glossary.aspx

Edition : BOD
ISBN-9782322132829
January 2017

A

a cappella - Sung without instrumental accompaniment.

AABA - The most common popular song form.

accent - A note or tone that is given stress by volume or attack.

acclaim - Enthusiastic approval. He won acclaim as a member of the samba jazz pioneers Sambalanço Trio and for his landmark recording Quarteto Novo with Hermeto Pascoal in 1967.

acid jazz - Music for dancing, first heard in the 1980s, that combines elements of soul jazz, funk, and hip hop, and mixes acoustic and electric instruments. (See also groove and club jazz.)...

acoustic - relating to the study of the physical properties of sound

ad lib - Also "ad libitum." A notation on written music that gives the performer freedom to vary the notes or tempo; in jazz it typically means to improvise freely.

African-American music - music created by African-American musicians. The ultimate significance of all this is that the experiments in jazz during the 1940s brought back to African-American music several structural principles and techniques rooted in African traditions -Kubik (2005).

afro - A rounded thickly curled hairdo. As the music has developed and spread around the world it has drawn on many different national, regional and local musical cultures giving rise, since its early 20th century American beginnings, to many distinctive styles: New Orleans jazz dating from the early 1910s, big band swing , Kansas City jazz and Gypsy jazz from the 1930s and 1940s, bebop from the mid-1940s and on down through West Coast jazz , cool jazz , avant-garde jazz , Afro-Cuban jazz , modal jazz , free jazz...

air check - A musical radio broadcast that was originally recorded for distribution to other stations; radio broadcasts that people have recorded off the radio that are sometimes released commercially or bootlegged.

all-in - The last chorus (in older jazz), often louder and more vigorous than the rest, and played by the ensemble.

alteration: The raising or lowering of a tone by a half-step, from its diatonic value in a chord. In Jazz usage, the fifth and ninth may be raised (augmented) or lowered (diminished); the fourth (or eleventh) may be augmented; the thirteenth may be diminished. The expression 'diminished seventh' is used solely as the name of a chord. Of course, in general music theory, any interval may be augmented or diminished.

altered chord - A dominant chord that has the 5th or 9th raised or lowered by a single semi-tone.

alternate takes - The various takes recorded of a piece of music at a single recording session, that for whatever reasons were not chosen to be used. (A version recorded on a different day is not an alternate take.)...

altissimo - very high

amplification - addition of extra material or illustration or clarifying detail

archetypal - of an original type after which other things are patterned

arco - Playing a string instrument with the bow, instead of pizzicato.

arpeggio - Sounding the individual notes of a chord quickly, one at a time, usually starting at the lowest note.

arrangement - An adaptation of a musical composition. Arrangements may be as minimal as a bass line or as complex as a full orchestral score. An arranger may take such great liberties with the original piece that it becomes a new composition.

arranger - A person who writes arrangements.

arrhythmic - Without an obvious beat.

Armstrong - United States pioneering jazz trumpeter and bandleader

articulation - The style in which a tone is produced, i.e., with slurs, staccato, variations in volume, and the like.

A Section: The first section of a tune, typically 8 bars; the main theme.

atonal - Without a tonal center.

attack - The manner in which a tone is articulated.

augmented: Raised by a half-step. See 'Alteration'.

avant-garde jazz - A term loosely applied to various forms of "experimental" jazz first heard in the 1950s, and their later offshoots, especially in the sixties and seventies (see free jazz)...

ax - Also "axe." Any musical instrument.

B

back beat - A rhythmic device 2 and 4 in 4/4 time in which the second and fourth beat of a measure is heavily emphasized in 4/4 time.

ballad - A slow song, usually of a romantic nature; sometimes used for any song of the AABA or similar popular song form.

balloon lungs - A brass man with plenty of wind. That cat must have "balloon lungs," Stix said he held that note for three and half minutes!"

bar - Also known as measure. A grouping of beats, that establishes the meter of a piece of music.

barn burner - Originally in Sinatra slang this was a stylish, classy woman, but today, it can even be applied to a good football game. Hey, Quincy, did you see Stella over at the diner? Man, she is one amazing "barn burner."

barre chord or bar chord - A guitar chord in which the first (or another finger) holds down two or more adjacent strings (that is it "bars" several notes)

barrelhouse - (1) An older style of piano, rough, loud, and appropriate to playing in noisy bars and dance halls. (2) Barrelhouse was the colloquial term for a cabaret in New Orleans where liquor was served. Barrelhouse music is the type of music played in one of these cabarets. Hey, Man, I dig this "barrelhouse" music. It flows free.

bass drum - Also "kick drum." The largest and lowest-pitched drum of the drum set, and played with a foot pedal.

bassline - The low-pitched instrumental part or line played by a rhythm section instrument (see also "line" below)

beat - (1) The pronounced rhythm of music. (2) One single stroke of a rhythmic accent

bebop - Also "bop." A style of jazz characterized by long flowing melodic lines, irregular accents, non-symmetrical written themes, and elaborated harmonies. The style of Jazz developed by young players in the early 40s, particularly Parker, Gillespie, Kenny Clarke, Charlie Christian and Bud Powell. Small groups were favored, and simple standard tunes or just their chord progressions were used as springboards for rapid, many-oted improvisations using long, irregular, syncopated phrasing. Improv was based on chordal harmony rather than the tune. The 'higher intervals' of the chords (9th, 11th and 13th) were emphasized in improv and in piano chord voicings, and alterations were used more freely than before, especially the flatted 5th & augmented 11th. The ground beat was moved from the bass drum to the ride cymbal and the string bass, and the rhythmic feel is more flowing and subtle than before. Instrumental virtuosity was stressed, while tone quality became more restrained, less obviously 'expressive'.

behind the beat - Playing slightly behind the beat as articulated by the rhythm section or implied by the ensemble.

bend - Jazz term referring either to establishing a pitch, sliding down half a step and returning to the original pitch or sliding up half a step from the original note. With the electric guitar, bending is widely used in blues, blues-rock, and rock and, to a somewhat different fashion, in jazz.

big band - An orchestra of more than 10 members.

birdbrain - A Charlie Parker imitator.It's 1957 already. We need something new. I'm gettin' tired of all of the "Birdbrains" around these days.

bitonality - The use of two different keys at once.

block chords - A style of piano playing, developed by Milt Buckner and George Shearing, with both hands 'locked' together, playing chords in parallel with the melody, usually in fairly close position. It is a technical procedure requiring much practice, and can sound dated if the harmonies are not advanced enough. Also called locked hands.

blow - To improvise (on any instrument); to play.

blowing changes - The chords of a tune, particularly those intended specifically for improvising which may vary somewhat from the changes of the head. Sometimes written on a separate page.

blue note, Blue Note - 1) the note in a blues scale that is dissonant with the other notes and thus produces a kind of tension when it is played (for those with some musical training, it is the flattened third or flattened fifth); 2) a well-loved Jazz label known especially for its *Hard Bop* recordings (see the entry for *Hard Bop* under Schools of Jazz at the end of this glossary)

blue notes - (1) Pitches in the scale that can be flattened or sharpened within the blues scale; (2) tones that are bent or changed to increase the expressivity of the music, not simply to alter the scale.

blues - (1) A 12-bar form built on the I, IV, and V chords; (2) a scale with a flatted third, fifth, and perhaps a seventh; (3) a poetic form; (4) a way of articulating tones; (5) a set of verbal...

body percussion - Playing sounds on the body such as claps, thumping the chest, patting thighs, or tapping two fingers in the palm of the hand.

bolero - Originally, a Cuban mid-tempo form played by guitar trios; now more generally a slower and more sentimental form (Latin).

bombs - Irregular bass drum accents (typical of bebop drummers).

boogaloo - Also bugalú. A rhythm and blues and soul-influenced Latin form originated in the United States and characterized by elements of mambo and chachachá with an added back beat.

boogie woogie - A style of piano playing very popular in the thirties. Blues, with continuous repeated eighth note patterns in the left hand and exciting but often stereotyped blues riffs and figures in the right hand.

book - The repertoire of a band or singer.

boot it - To play with energy and excitement (early jazz).

bootleg - Recordings or made or sold without the permission of the performers or a recording company.

bop - See bebop.

bossa nova - A Brazilian jazz/pop music form derived from the samba (originated c. 1960), influenced by cool jazz, and usually played quietly, with minimal percussion.

bounce - A light, medium fast tempo piece (swing era).

box - A piano; a guitar.

brass bands - Primarily from New Orleans, these groups play instruments that can be carried. Brass bands play in parades and jazz funerals and improvise as they march.

break - A short suspension of rhythm or the flow of the music (usually of a four or eight beat duration) while the soloist or melody instruments continue playing.

bridge - The third group of eight-bars in a thirty-two bar chorus (see popular song form); also known as the channel, the middle-eight or the B-section.

bring down or bringdown - As a verb - to depress. As a noun - one who depresses.Hey, man, don't "bring me down" with all of this crazy talk.Hey, let's get out of here, that guy is a real "bringdown."

broken time - A way of playing in which the beat is not stated explicitly. Irregular, improvised syncopation. Especially applied to bass and drum playing.

brushes - Drum sticks with wire brushes on the end, sued to produce a quieter, scratching sound.

B Section: See bridge.

C

call-and-response - An antiphonal pattern common to jazz and all African American folk music, with a "call" played by a soloist and "answered" by the ensemble.

chachacha - Also "chachachá." A mambo and/or danzón-derived rhythmic style and dance form (Latin).

cadence - A key-establishing chord progression, generally following the circle of fifths. A turnaround is one example of a cadence. Sometimes a whole section of a tune can be an extended cadence. In understanding the harmonic structure of a tune, it's important to see which chords are connected to which others in cadences.

call and response - A musical conversation led by one singer or instrumentalist and with a response from another singer or instrumentalist. You can think of it as a musical question and answer.

CESH - Contrapuntal Elaboration of Static Harmony, a foolish term used in some Jazz textbooks. The use of moving inner voices to give propulsion to a chord that lasts for a while.

changes - A series of chords; the harmonic structure of a piece of music; the chords for a particular melody.

channel - An old term for the bridge.

charanga - Originally a Cuban orchestra of a flute, violins, and rhythm section, now more often with brass instruments added.

Charleston rhythm - a dance rhythm from the 1920s, consisting of two emphatic beats followed by a rest.

chart - (1) Any musical score. (2) A special type of score, used by Jazz musicians. Only the melody line, words (if any) and chord symbols are given. Clef, key signature and meter are given once only, at the beginning. The standards of musical notation and calligraphy are low. Details are often scanty or inaccurate, which encourages the musician to amend and elaborate the chart for his own purposes. Every Jazz musician has his own book of miscellaneous charts.

chase - A series of short musical passages (trading fours or twos) played by several players at a fast tempo.

Chicago style jazz - A style of small band jazz popular in Chicago in the 1920s and 1930s that derived from New Orleans style, but emphasized greater solo space, fixed ensembles, and a more prominent role for the rhythm section.

chops - A slang term which refers to a player's strong technique or endurance, Technical ability, to execute music physically and to negotiate chord changes. Distinct from the capacity to have good ideas, to phrase effectively and build a solo. ("That alto sax player has great chops; she can play for hours.")

chord - The harmony at a given moment. Loosely, a group of 3 or more notes played together. Strictly, a chord is the basic unit of harmony, regarded abstractly as having a given root and specifying some other tones at certain intervals from the root, without regard to the actual voicing of the notes on the piano (see Voicing and Scale).

chord progression - See changes.

chorus - The refrain or the main body of a popular song. See popular song forms.

chromatic scale - A sequence of all twelve notes in an octave, played in a row (either ascending or descending). Fragments of the chromatic scale are used in many styles of popular music, but more extensive use of chromatic scale tends to occur in jazz, fusion, and the more experimental genres of rock.

chromaticism - The use of all 12 tones of a scale...

circle of fifths - A series of twelve perfect fifths that circle back to the original tone.

circular breathing - A technique used by wind instrument players and singers to produce a continuous stream of notes without stopping for air. (The air is inhaled through the nose simultaneously while the mouth continues to produce musical sounds.)...

clave - A five-beat pattern that underlies all salsa music.

claves - A pair of wooden sticks used to play the clave pattern (Latin).

close voicing: One in which the chord tones are bunched together, generally within an octave range.

coda - (1) A portion of a tune which seems like a tail, or extra measures, added to the last A section. It is repeated for every chorus, however. (2) An ending for a tune, used only once after the final chorus. There is often confusion in written charts as to whether a coda is 'every time' or 'out-chorus only'. Some charts, to save space, are written so that the tune appears to have a coda, but it's really just a normal part of the tune.

collective improvisation - Simultaneous improvisation by several musicians (most often heard in early jazz and free jazz).

combo - A small instrumental group of fewer than ten musicians.

comping - The pattern of rhythmic placement of harmony used by keyboardists and guitarists while accompanying soloists.

conjunto - "Combo": a band of guitar, tres, bass, bongos, trumpets, piano, percussion, and three vocalists, first formed for playing in Cuban carnival (Latin).

consonance - a combination of notes that sound pleasant when played together (see also *dissonance*)

contrapuntal - See counterpoint.

cool: The style of the early 50s, taken up by many white musicians and popular on college campuses. The basis was bebop, but the fastest tempos were not used and the sound was quiet and understated. Miles Davis was one of the main originators.

cool jazz - A jazz style characterized by moderate volume, quiet rhythm sections, low vibrato, and sometimes improvised counterpoint; c. 1950s. (See also West Coast jazz.)...

coro - "Chorus": the two or three-voice refrain sung against a montuno.

coro/pregón - Call-and-response between soloist and the coro (Latin). \...

counterpoint - Independent improvised or composed melodies played against each other.

counting off: Giving the tempo and meter by counting aloud.

cross rhythm - The simultaneous use of two or more different rhythmic patterns; a basic feature of most African American musics.

crush: On the piano, a half-step played simultaneously.

cut/cutting/carving - To outplay other musicians, usually in a jam session.

D

danzon - Also danzón. A 19th century Cuban dance derived from European contredances; a musical form usually played by a charanga (Latin).

descarga - A Latin jam session.

diatonic - The contrary of 'chromatic'. Said of melody or harmony using only the unaltered major (or sometimes minor) scale.

dig - To appreciate a player's expression.

diminished - Lowered by a half-step. See 'Alteration'.

diminished triad - Triad composed of two stacked minor thirds, root, minor third, and diminished fifth.

diminished seventh (°7) - Chord composed of 4 notes, stacked in minor thirds. The symbol is a small raised circle. Since an additional minor third on top will be the octave of the bottom note, inversions of a °7 will have the same interval structure in other words, they will also be diminished 7th chords in their own right. The extensions of a °7 are a ninth (or whole step) above each chord tone. Effective modern voicing requires using at least one extension; plain °7 chords sound remarkably old-fashioned. If the chord tones and extensions are put together within an octave, the diminished scale results. Often called just 'diminished' with '7th' being implied.

dirty tone - A description used in the in the 1920s and 1930s for horn players with a rough, noisy tone quality.

dissonance - a combination of notes that sound harsh when played together. Artful insertion of dissonances is one way to build tension musically and is frequently used in jazz music. (See also *consonance*.)

Dixieland - Also "Dixie." a sub-genre of jazz also known as *New Orleans Jazz*.

dot time - A cross-rhythm based on dotted quarter notes, extending through a passage.

double - The ability to play more than one instrument.

double-time - A doubling of tempo in the melody while the accompanying instruments remain at the slower tempo; or all the instruments doubling the tempo together. This is a common rhythm device in ballad playing.

double time feel - A time feel twice as fast, so that written eighth notes now sound like quarter notes, while the chords continue at the same speed as before.

bown by law - is to have paid dues; that is, to have earned respect for your talent or ability to "get down."Charlie Parker spent years on the road working a lot of dives to fine-tune his craft. He earned every bit of success and recognition he later received. He was "down by law."

down-home - Music that is honest, folk-like, and possibly funky.

downbeat - The first beat of a measure.

drone - Another name for pedal point.

drop - Jazz term referring to a note that slides chromatically downwards to an indefinite pitch .

drum set - Also "drum kit." A collection of drums, cymbals, and various other percussion instruments played by a single drummer; includes a bass drum, tom-toms, snare drum, hi-hat cymbal, ride cymbal, etc.

dub - A copy of another recording.

dynamics - Different degrees of volume and intensity.

E

EAI - Electroacoustic improvisation; a term that may be used to include such styles and processes also known as "reductionist," "Onkyo," "minimal," and "lowercase" improvised music.

ear, play by - Playing an instrument without written music.

eight-to-the-bar - Continuous eighth-note rhythm, as in boogie-woogie left hand patterns.

extended harmony - Notes added to a chord beyond the octave, for example, 9th, 11th, and 13th chords.

extensions - The ninth, eleventh and thirteenth of a chord.

F

fake - To play without written music.

fake book - A collection of Jazz charts, published without paying royalties and thus illegal (not in the Public Domain.) For decades, a book called '1000 Standard Tunes' circulated; you can still see its grossly simplified charts, written three to a page. Some 25 years ago the "Real Book" appeared, out of the Berklee School of Music, with some 400 tunes in excellent calligraphy. This has become the standard and all Jazz musicians are expected to have a copy. More recently a number of legal fake books have been published. The best is The Ultimate Jazz Fakebook.

false fingering - A technique of altered finger placement that produces tones or density of sound on horns that are not available by orthodox techniques.

feedback - The resonance loop created when a microphone or guitar pickup is placed close to a highly amplified speaker, often creating a howling or screeching sound. In most cases, musicians and sound engineers seek to avoid feedback with microphones and acoustic instruments; with electric guitar, especially in heavy metal and shred guitar playing it may be done on purpose.

fills - Short improvised passages behind a soloist or between sections of a piece of music.

finger Zinger - Someone who plays very fast.Ignasio the new guitarist is a finger zinger on the guitar. Damn, that boy is incredible!

flag waver - A spectacular (and usually up-tempo) piece of music (swing era).

flatted fifth - The lowering (by a half-step) of the fifth degree of a chord; a device especially associated with early bebop.

flip - A verb meaning to go crazy or a noun meaning an eccentric. That dude is really cooking, I think he's going to "flip."

flip your lid - Same as "Blow your top." That cat looks crazy. I think he's gonna "flip his lid."

fly - Smooth or slick. Hey, Eddie, did you see the hat-check girl Bernice? Man, she is "fly.".

formulaic improvisation - The use of a wide variety of elements (including favorite licks or fragments, manipulations of intervals and range, interpolated phrases, etc.) in developing a solo.

four-beat - Also playing in four. A form of rhythm organization in which all four beats are relatively equal. Four-beat was especially common in the swing era and afterwards, but was also found in earlier jazz.

freak Lip - A pair of kissers that wear like leather; one who can hit high C's all night and play a concert the next day. Ol' Satchmo... now he had a pair of "freak lips!"

free - Without rules. Especially, improvising without regard to the chord changes, or without any chord changes. Usually there is an implied restriction in 'free' playing preventing one from sounding as if chord changes are being used.

free jazz - A cluster of jazz styles (post-1954) that minimize the importance of a fixed beat and a given harmonic structure, and emphasize the sound and texture of music.

front line - The horns; all the instruments but the rhythm section.

funk - Also "funky." A loose term for music that draws from blues- or gospel-based harmony, rhythm, and melody; also (since the 1960s) a complex, bass and rhythm guitar-driven, sometimes three-against-four pattern, with horns used in rhythm patterns and shouted vocals.

fusion - A style developed in the late 60s by Wayne Shorter, Herbie Hancock, Miles Davis, Chick Corea and others, partly as a reaction to the eclipse of Jazz on the music scene by rock. Incorporated elements of rock into Jazz and made greater use of repetition and non-improvised passages. Harmonic language was simplified; key feeling tended to be established by repetition rather than harmonic movement. Straight-8 time and a strong back-beat predominated.

G

ghost note - A note that is fingered on a wind instrument but blown so lightly as to be inaudible; on a musical transcription, a note that may or may not be in the original.

glissando - Sliding or slurring from one note to the next quickly.

goof - Fail to carry out a responsibility or wander in attention.Hey, Leroy, stop "goofin'" when I'm talkin' to ya.

go out - Take the final chorus, end.

grand staff - The treble and bass staves together.

groove - An infectious feeling of rightness in the rhythm, of being perfectly centered. This is a difficult term to define. A Medium Groove is a tempo of, say, 112, with a slinky or funky feeling.

groovy - Used in the fifties to denote music that swings or is funky. For a short while in the sixties, groovy was synonymous with cool. The word has been used little since the seventies.Hey, Jack, dig that "groovy" beat.

ground beat - The basic metric beat, most often in quarter-notes, whether explicitly stated or not.

guajeo - A riff played by the strings in a charanga, or the tres in a conjunto; also repeated horn lines (Latin).

gutbucket - Gutbucket refers to something to store liquor in and to the type of music associated with heavy drinking. An early term for lowdown or earthy music. That cat Satchmo started out playing some real "gutbucket" in the houses down in New Orleans.

H

half-diminished ($^\varnothing$) - The chord with a minor third, a lowered (diminished) fifth, and a minor seventh. Formally called 'minor 7 flat 5'. This chord probably evolved from the IV minor 6th chord, which was common in the swing period; if its sixth is taken to be the root, a half-diminished chord results. The symbol is a small O with a diagonal slash. It is most often the harmony of the ii in a ii-V-I progression in a minor key. Two different scales have been commonly used for this chord; one with a flat 9th, the 'locrian', and one with an unflatted ninth, the latter scale being more modern.

half-time - A rhythmic device in which the melody continues at a fixed tempo while the accompanying instruments double the tempo.

half time feel: A time feel half as fast, while the chords go by in the same amount of time. Occurs in the intro to Chick Corea's Tones for Joan's Bones.

hard bop - The style of the late 50s, engineered by Horace Silver, Art Blakey, etc. Still essentially Bebop, the style used hard-driving rhythmic feel and vehement, biting lines and harmony drenched with urban blues, rhythm 'n blues and gospel. Original compositions were stressed over the old standards used in Bebop, ranging from simple riff-based blues to elaborate compositions, sometimes using whole-tone scales. Hard Bop had a black, street flavor, a reaction, in part, to the intellectuality of the Cool School.

harmonic rhythm - The structural organization of chord progressions in time; the rate at which the chords pass by. Since this may not be related to the rhythms of the actual notes, it is an abstract concept.

harmony - Simultaneous sounding of two or more tones.

have a ball - to enjoy oneself enormously.

head - The first (and last) chorus of a tune, in which the song or melody is stated without improvisation or with minimal improvisation.

head arrangement - A musical arrangement made up (usually collectively) during a performance.

hi-hat cymbal - Two cymbals on a single rod that snap together when operated by a foot pedal.

hip (or hep) - Keenly aware of or knowledgeable about life's developments, especially in the arts. "Hipness is what it is. But sometimes hipness is what it ain't..."

hipster (or Hepster) - One who is Hip (or Hep.) A follower of the various genres of bop jazz in the 50's. These were the precursors of hippies in the 60's. Those "hipsters" that hang out at Shelly's Manne-Hole are really diggin' the West Coast sound.

hocket - The division of a melody into separate parts for different voices or instruments, resulting in a kind of cross-talk.

homophony - A musical texture with one voice (or melody line) accompanied by chords; also used as an adjective (homophonic). Compare with polyphony, in which several voices or melody lines are performed at the same time.

honk - A low note played loudly on a reed instrument. (See also overblowing).

horn - A wind instrument; or any instrument.

horn section - In a jazz, blues, or R&B context, this refers to a small group of brass players who accompany an ensemble by playing soft "pads" and punctuating the melodic line with "punches" (sudden interjections).

hot - Hot jazz (as distinct from the music of sweet bands or commercial music) was a name for early jazz.

I

improvisation - Music created in the moment of performance, without written scores or played from memory.

interlude - An additional section in a tune, especially one between one person's solo and another's. The Dizzy Gillespie standard A Night In Tunisia has a famous interlude.

interpolations - See quote.

interval - The distance between two tones.

intro (introduction) - A composed section at the beginning of a tune, heard only once.

inversion - (1) In traditional music theory, a chord with a note other than the root in the bass. (2) With regard to any particular voicing, especially a left-hand rootless voicing, a rearrangement of the voicing by moving the bottom note up an octave. Or, any one octavewise arrangement of a voicing.

J

jam session - Also "jamming." The most informal of jazz arrangements, and one which depends solely on the shared knowledge of the players. It was once a common practice among jazz musicians, often occurring after hours, in clubs or spaces set aside for…

jazz - (1) A style of American music that originated in New Orleans circa 1900, characterized by strong, prominent meter, improvisation, distinctive tone colors and performance techniques, and dotted or syncopated rhythmic patterns. (2) In a big band chart, a rhythm indication for medium to up-tempo swing (as opposed to latin).

jazz critic - Someone who reviews jazz recordings or concerts and writes about them in newspapers, magazines, and books. Often critics influence people to buy or not buy recordings.

jazz standard - A well-known tune by a Jazz musician. See Standard.

Jitterbug - A jumpy, jittery energetic dance or one who danced this dance during the swing period.Artie Shaw is a hot clarinet player. He sure has all of the "jitterbugs" jumpin'.

jive - A versatile word which can be used as a noun, verb or adjective. Noun - an odd form of speech. Verb - to fool someone. Adjective - phoney or fake.Old Satchmo can lay down some crazy "jive." Don't "jive"me man, I wasn't born yesterday. That cat is one "jive" dude.

jump - Also "jump band." A sub-style of swing played by small bands in the late 1930s and 1940s that combined strong rhythms, riff tunes, blues, and pop songs. A precursor to rhythm and blues.

K

Kansas City style - Pre-swing and swing music from Midwestern and Southwestern bands that emphasized larger ensembles, saxophone sections, the blues, riff melodies, and strong walking bass.

key - A scale; the first note of a scale.

kick it off - To set a tempo and start a performance by "stomping" it off, or otherwise signaling it.

killer-diller - An exciting (or difficult to play) piece of music (swing era).

L

lame - Something that doesn't quite cut it. Some of the cats that claim to be playin' Jazz these days are layin' down some "lame" music.

lay back - To create an effect by falling behind the rhythm.

lay out - A jazz term which is the equivalent of the classical term *tacet*; it instructs the player to cease playing for a section or tune.

lead - The melody or top part of an arrangement; a part played by a lead trumpet, lead alto saxophone, etc.

lead sheet - A form of music notation that specifies the melody & harmony (and sometimes the lyric) of a tune. The melody is written in modern Western music notation and the harmony is specified with chord symbols above the staff. A single selection from a Fake Book is also referred to as a lead sheet. Also see "Chart".

left hand/right hand - A distinction made by drummers' and pianists' for the use of different hands.

left hand rootless voicing ('LHRV') - A close-position voicing without a root, played mainly in the octave of middle C. In a style perfected by Bill Evans, these left-hand chords are sprinkled in irregular syncopations under the right-hand melody. The absence of roots both frees the bass player and allows a richer harmony in the voicing. This has become the mainstream style of left-hand playing.

legit - The Jazz musician's somewhat ironic term for music, or a gig, that is not Jazz.

legato - Performing with a minimal break between tones.

licks - (1) An early term for phrase or solo. Louie can really lay down some "hot licks." (2) Short musical ideas that are regularly repeated in the improvisations of a particular soloist. See formulaic improvisation.

lindy hop - Also "Jitterbug." A popular dance that drew on a number of African American popular dances, including tap, the Charleston, the Texas Tommy, and others, and reached its peak in the 1930s and 1940s. It was a form of choreographed swing,...

line - A melody; one of the voices, such as bass line or melody line...

line-up - The personnel of a band.

lip - The strength and ability of brass players to execute music, especially high notes.

locked hands - A form of chord voicing for piano in which the left and right hands of a pianist moving together closely and in parallel, the left hand doubling the same chord played by the right. (See also block chords.)...

long meter - A chart in 4/4 time is said to be written in long meter when a written eighth-note feels like a quarter-note, and a written half-measure feels like a whole measure. In this way, for example, a 64-bar tune can be written as if it were a 32-bar tune, which may make it easier to read. The term, though useful, is little-known.

lydian - A major scale or chord with a raised 4th; the mode of the major scale built on 4. Regarded as the most fundamental Jazz scale by influential theorist George Russell.

lydian dominant - A dominant 7th scale with a raised 4th (11th). One of the fundamental forms of the dominant chord; also sometimes called 'lydo-mixian'. The scale/chord most appropriate for non-V dominants, such as II7 or bVII7.

M

mainstream jazz - The style of Jazz regarded by the average player as today's norm, as opposed to fusion, rock, avant-garde, etc.; sometimes the term implies a somewhat conservative, relatively diatonic vocabulary exemplified by Oscar Peterson. Mainstream Jazz is in a highly evolved state, having incorporated virtually the entire harmonic language of 20th century tonal music. In timbre, phrasing, form and rhythmic feel mainstream Jazz still rests on a basis of Bebop, which is why 'modern' Jazz is considered to have started with Bebop in the early 40s.

mambo - A musical section added to the danzón form in the 1940s; a musical form with heavy jazz influence developed in the 1940s and 1950s (Latin).

matrix number - Numbers and letters stamped near the center of a 78 RPM recording indicate the number of the take on the record.

measure - A grouping of beats, which indicates the meter of a particular piece of music. (See also bar).

medium tempo - One of the standard Jazz tempos, neither 'up' nor 'ballad'.

melisma - Melodic ornamentation by the use of more than one tone in singing a syllable.

melodic minor - In Jazz, a scale with a minor 3rd but a major 6th and 7th (both up and down). This scale and its modes (Altered, Half-diminished and Lydian Dominant are the familiar ones) make up a realm called melodic minor harmony. Also called 'tonic minor'.

melody - Specifically, the topmost line or voice.

meter - A basic music term, but sometimes not fully understood. The organization of the beats of time (or ground beat), moving at a certain rate (the tempo), into groupings which are heirarchical, that is, there is a unit of a stated number of beats (the bar) which includes strong and weak beats in an organized pattern. All this is implied by a 'meter' of 4/4, 3/4, etc.

microtone - An interval smaller than a half tone.

MIDI - Musical Instrument Digital Interface: An electronic standard by which musical information can be exchanged between synthesizers and computers.

modal jazz - (1) Said of a section, or a whole tune, having static harmony (using one chord) and using scales from a particular mode, most typically the Dorian. (2) Having a key feeling derived not from dynamic chord progressions (like circle-of-fifths) but rather from repetition, monotony, and weight. (3) Loosely, a harmonic style that is diatonic and makes use of quartal harmony.

mode - An incarnation of a scale in which a certain note is taken as the root. Thus, each scale has as many different modes as it has different tones. In common usage, the major scale and the melodic minor scale are regarded as 'given' and the scales constructed with other notes as the root are called modes. The modes of the major scale have names (Ionian, Dorian, Phrygian, Lydian, Mixolydian, Aeolian, and Locrian); these names were applied in the Renaissance and have no relationship to the Greek originals. Some of the melodic minor scale's modes have names in today's theory: mode 3, the augmented major 7th; mode 4, the lydian dominant; mode 6, the half-diminished; mode 7, the altered.

modern - The styles of Jazz since 1945. Especially applied to Bebop, Cool Jazz, and Hard Bop.

modulation - The establishment of a new key. This is mainly a matter of harmonic progression, but expectation, emphasis and phrasing also enter into determining whether a new key has really been established. In standards, a modulation to the beginning of the bridge is strongly expected. Typically, a II - V or a iii - VI - ii - V progression in the new key is used.

moldy fig - A term used by the Beboppers to deride players and fans of older styles, especially trad. Someone whose tastes are not up to date.

montuno - A term of Latin music which crops up in other Jazz. (1) An indefinitely repeated pattern of 1, 2 or 4 bars in the piano, typically with ingeniously syncopated moving inner voices and a differently syncopated bass line. (2) Incorrectly, a pyramiding vamp in which one instrument enters alone, then another is added, and so on at regular intervals.

motivic improvisation - The use of a few short fragments or elements of melody in developing a solo.

moving inner voice - A momentarily prominent line played by a voice in between the melody and the bass.

muggles - One nickname for marijuana used by early Jazzmen (Armstrong has a song by this title).Hey, Louis, I need to calm down. You got any "muggles?

multi-instrumentalism - Playing instruments of different types as a means of expanding a musician's creative possibilities...

multiphonics - A wind instrument or vocal technique by which more than one tone is produced simultaneously. (See also overblowing.)...

mutes, hats - Devices placed over the bell of a brass instrument for altering or softening the tone.

N

neck - On a guitar (e.g. acoustic guitar, electric guitar, electric bass), violin-family instrument (e.g. violin, upright bass) or other stringed instrument, the neck is the long, thin piece of wood which extends from the soundbox or body of the instrument and upon which the strings are put under tension between the bridge (on a guitar family instrument) or the tailpiece (on a violin-family instrument) and the headstock (for guitars) or the tuning pegs (violin) or machine heads (upright bass). The neck on acoustic and electric guitars and most electric basses has metal frets which divide the neck into semitones. Violin family instruments and fretless electric basses do not have frets.

Neo-bop - The conservative Bebop style of several successful players in the 90s, like Roy Hargrove.

New Orleans style - Jazz that developed in the early part of the 20th century in New Orleans and rural Louisiana. These styles were variously characterized by collective improvisation, homophony, two-beat and four-beat rhythms, leads passed from one horn to another, clarinet countermelodies, tailgate...

new thing, the - A term first used to describe free jazz, c. 1961.

nonet - An orchestra of nine performers, or a piece written for such a group.

noodling - To just play notes that have no particular meaning to a tune or solo.Quit "noodlin" cat, let's start working the tune.

note-for-note solo - A live or recorded performance by an instrumentalist which reproduces a previously recorded improvised solo. In some cases, the recreation of the previously recorded solo may be faithful down to the smallest nuances, such as the use of "whammy bar" embellishments and "ghost notes".

nu-jazz (also **electronica, jazztronica, future jazz,** or **electro-jazz)** - A loose term for music that combines live instruments played in jazz style with electronic elements (especially those in the beat); a style developed in the 1990s...

O

obbligato - An accompanying melody played by an instrument that fills behind a vocal or another instrumentalist. (Singer Jimmy Rushing once said, "You know the obbligato the horns play behind the singer? Bebop is the obbligato without the singer.")...

open voicing - One in which the chord tones are spread out over a greater range.

organ chords - Basic chords, similar to those used in simple hymns.

original - A tune composed by a Jazz musician and played by him but perhaps not well-known to others.

ostinato - A melodic phrase that is repeated again and again in the same pitches.

out - The last chorus of a tune, when the head is played for the last time. On the stand the gesture of a raised clenched fist or a finger pointing to the head indicates that the out chorus is coming up.

outer voice - The melody line or the bass, the top or bottom line.

outro - A jocular term for coda; an added ending section.

outside/inside, playing - (1) The A sections of a tune, the parts other than the bridge. (2) A manner of playing over changes that avoids using the normal scales, or has no relationship to the changes. (3) A style of playing without using conventional Jazz chords.

overblowing - A wind instrument technique in which increased air pressure is combined with lip manipulation to extend the range of the horn and produce a variety of tones. (See also multiphonics.)...

P

pachanga - A rhythmic style and a dance developed in the 1950s and 1960s.

pantonal - Another name for atonality.

paraphrase improvisation - Decorating and reworking a melody or parts of a melody in different forms.

passing tone - A non-harmonic note that connects other notes that are harmonic...

pattern - A pre-planned melodic figure, repeated at different pitch levels. Something played automatically by the fingers without much thought. Reliance on patterns is the hallmark of a weak player.

"Payin' your dues" - Playing or singing for free or little money, also playing boring or non-jazz related jobs that were done to make money only. Sometimes playing with a group that is not as good as you. It takes time to get well-known and to advance to the level where you no longer have to accept boring or low-paying jobs to make it big in the jazz world.

P-bass - An abbreviation for the Fender Precision bass, a widely used brand of electric bass

pedal - A bass line that stays mainly on one note (or its octaves) under several changes of harmony. Also pedal-point. The most typical situation is when a dominant pedal (bass on V) underlies a turnaround progression like I - VI - ii - V. The root of the I chord can also act as a pedal.

pedal point - A method of playing in which a song or section of a song is not built on chord *changes*, but on a single, repeated bass note. *Pedal point* tends to have a hypnotic effect and is often used in *Modal* jazz

pentatonic - Pertaining to scales of 5 notes to the octave, in particular 1-2-3-5-6 of the major scale. Pentatonic melodies are typical of much indigenous music around the world, and these scales are also an important part of the modern Jazz sound. Pentatonic melodies and patterns were especially typical of Jazz and fusion in the seventies.

perfect fifth - An interval of seven semitones.

phrase - A natural break or unit in a melody line, similar in function to a clause in a sentence.

pickup notes - The notes leading into a tune or a chorus.

pizzicato - The plucking of strings with the fingers.

pocket - In the pocket means perfectly in time, especially bass playing that is 'in the center' of the beat (rather than slightly leading or dragging the beat).

polyphony - Music of several different melodic parts that support each other.

polyrhythm - Simultaneous use of different meters.

polytonality - The use of two different keys simultaneously. Despite much loose talk, true polytonality is rare. Upper structures (q.v.) and outside playing do not usually qualify because there is always a strong single underlying tonality.

popular song forms - The American popular song form derives from a long history of European folk song, theater music, and light opera, and was modified in America by Broadway musicals, African American folk songs, the blues, and other musics. The most common popular...

popsicle stick - A sax player's reed. I'm playing a great popsicle stick.

post-bop - A general term for many developments in jazz after the 1950s.

press roll - A drum roll (borrowed from marching band drumming) formed by a series of double-strokes of the drum sticks; the press roll is often used to end a phrase, or bring in or help a soloist exit.

progression - A definite series of chords, forming a passage with some harmonic unity or dramatic meaning. One speaks of the progressions that crop up repeatedly in different tunes, and studies how to negotiate them. Chords in progressions are labelled with Roman numerals (I, II, etc.) while scale degrees, and upper structures (q.v.), are labelled with arabic numerals (1, 2, etc.).

progressive jazz - Modern jazz (c. 1945-1955); also music associated with the Stan Kenton Orchestra.

pulse - The basic beat of a performance...

Q

quadrille - Sets of dances popular in the 19th century, often said to be one of the roots of jazz.

quote - A snatch of some other well-known tune thrown into a solo. A good quote is unexpected, incongruous and yet seems to fit perfectly. Some quotes are cliches, as 'Grand Canyon Suite' in 'All the Things You Are'.

R

race records - Recordings produced in the 1920s-30s exclusively for African American audiences.

ragtime - A piano, vocal, and band music form (c. 1890 and later) with syncopated melodies played over regular rhythmic emphasis in a left-hand bass moving at half the melodies' speed.

refrain - The chorus at the end of every stanza in some pop songs (see pop song forms).

register - A name for different parts of a vocalist's or an instrument's range.

remote key - A key distant on the circle of fifths from the original one, such as E major compared to C major.

rhumba (or rumba) - A Cuban musical form of various styles (Latin) based on the son.

rhythm and blues - Also "R&B." The adaptation of blues to small bands with wind instruments, and the merging of blues with riff melodies, and pop songs.

rhythm changes - The chord progression for George Gershwin's "I Got Rhythm"; commonly used as a basis for improvisation.

rhythm section - The instruments that function to provide the rhythmic foundation of a jazz group (bass, drums, keyboards, rhythm guitar, etc.) The contrast is to the saxophone section and brass sections).

ride cymbal - A medium-sized cymbal that produces a loud and shimmering sound, and is used to set the fundamental swing pulse of most jazz performances.

riff - (1) A relatively simple, catchy repeated phrase. May be played behind a soloist or as part of a head. Often in a bluesy style. Riff tunes are made up of riffs, characteristic of the black bands of the 30s. (2) A pre-packaged phrase used by an improviser when he can't think of anything else, especially one which is especially catchy.

root -The fundamental pitch on which a chord is based, from which the chord takes its name, and to which the other tones of the chord are referred to intervallically the third, seventh, and so on, regardless of their actual intervallic relationship in an actual keyboard voicing. Note that the root is often absent in Jazz piano, both in voicings and in r.h. patterns and lines. This avoidance of the obvious is part of the character of Jazz.

rhythm Changes - The chords to 'I Got Rhythm' (Gershwin), somewhat modified and simplified. Many

Jazz tunes use these changes and every player must know them. There are several variations.

rhythm Section - The piano, bass and drums in a combo, those who play throughout the tune, behind the soloists. Might also include guitar or vibes, or there might be no piano.

rim shot - The sharp, loud sound made by a stick striking the head and the rim of a snare drum simultaneously.

rip - A quick upward glissando up to an intended tone.

roll - A sustained sound on the drums produced by fast alternate strokes of the drum sticks.

run - A rapid descending, or ascending, usually right-hand passage on the piano in the form of a continuous scale, or a scale with variations.

S

salsa - A hot, up-tempo U.S. blend of Cuban, jazz, Panamanian, and Puerto Rican musics.

sample or sampling - To record a short portion from a live performance or from a recording of an instrument or group, so that this short "snippet" can be re-played or re-used in another performance or recording. In the 2000s, sampling is usually done by making a digital recording of the desired sample. Sampling is widely used in 2000s-era pop, hip-hop, and electronica.

sampler - An electronic device that allows an analog sound to be captured, digitally converted, and played back by an electronic instruments such as the keyboards or guitar.

scale - (1) A selection of tones in the octave, arranged in ascending or descending order, usually but not always using intervals of half- or whole-steps, and using the same notes in every successive octave. One tone is usually thought of as being the root, but it need not be the first note played. Most scales have 5, 6, 7 or 8 notes to the octave but any number from 2 to 12 is possible. (2) The same group of tones regarded abstractly as a 'pool' of available notes. In this sense, scale really means the same as chord. There is a maxim: 'Scales are chords and chords are scales.' (3) A section of melody in the form of a scale.

scat - Improvise lyrics as nonsense syllables. Said to have originated on the "Hot Five" song "Heebie Jeebies" when Louis Armstrong dropped his lyrics.I can really dig Dizzy's new way of singing "scat."

scratch - In a recording context, this refers to a rough "scratch track", which is the recording of a rhythm section part or vocals which is done to provide a temporary reference point for the performers who will be recording their parts (the "scratch track" is erased later on; in the context of hip-hop music and turntablism, "scratching" refers to the manipulation of a vinyl record on a turntable with the hands and a DJ mixer to create rhythmic sounds.

second - The interval between two adjacent scale tones.

second line - The dancing crowd that follows a marching band in New Orleans; a rhythm associated with New Orleans street bands.

semitone - Half of the interval of a whole tone.

septet - a jazz group with seven members

septeto - An Cuban orchestra developed in the late 1920s by adding a trumpet to a sexteto (Latin).

sequencer - An electronic device that stores a series of tones to be played back later. An entire performance or composition can be built up from such sequences that have been stored and manipulated.

sextet - a jazz group with six members

sexteto - A Cuban orchestra from 1920 with tres, guitar, bass, bongos, maracas, and claves (Latin).

shake - Extreme vibrato on a brass instrument.

shed - Short for Woodshed, to practice diligently. Also "shedding." See woodshed.

shout chorus - A special, complete, through-composed chorus played just before the final out-chorus. Used in classic (20s) Jazz, some bebop, and a few modern compositions, such as Wayne Shorter's This Is For Albert.

shuffle - A rhythm used in earlier jazz, based on uneven triplets, and deriving from a dance step in which the feet move across the floor without being lifted.

side-slipping - To play a passage, a melody or chord, a half-step up or down from its expected place or in relation to the given harmony.

sidefills - A slang term for onstage monitor speakers that are placed on the sides of the stage, to help performers to hear themselves.

sideman - Any member of a band or small group other than the leader.

sides - Records.We sat around and dug "sides." Or, as George Crater (or was it Ira Gitler?) once put it, "I sat around with another musician and Doug Sides." ~ Bob Blumenthal

skins player - The drummer. (Skins comes from the days when cowhide or other dried animal skin was used to make drum heads.)Man, we were all ready to have a little improv jam session but our "skins player" skipped out on us. There's one cat that I'm gonna skin!

slap-tongue - An popping effect created by striking the tongue against the mouthpiece of a reed instrument (early jazz).

smear - A rough, often loud slide away from a tone.

smokin' - Playing your ass off.I can already tell from outside that Jimmy is "smokin'" tonight.

smooth jazz - A later development of fusion in which elements of rhythm and blues and pop music were distilled and refined by the formulas and constraints of radio to become bright and recognizable melodies (though ironically often recorded with audiophile sensibilities in...

snake - A slang term which refers to an audio multicore cable that terminates in a patchbay; it is used to route the signals of all of the onstage microphones and instrument amplifiers to the mixing board at the back of the performance venue.

sock cymbal - A large cymbal, often used for the heaviest accents.

solo - Any one player's improvisation over one or more choruses of the tune (occasionally, especially in ballads, less than one chorus). A sharp distinction is made between soloing, and playing the head.

son - A classic Cuban dance and song form originated near the turn of the 20th century and continued and varied in modern Cuban-derived pop music (Latin).

song form - A musical form with two contrasting themes A and B, thus-- A (8 bars); A repeated; B (8 bars); A repeated. The three A's have slightly different endings (turnarounds). Another common form may be called song form also, ABAB' (the second B starting like the first but ending differently). Most older standards are in song form.

soul jazz - One of the musics included under the name of hard bop (c. mid- to late 1950s). It uses speech-inflected tonality, folk, blues or church-based melodies and rhythms (frequently 6/8), the electric organ, and other elements identified with funk.

stand - The bandstand or stage.

standard - A tune universally accepted and played by many Jazz musicians. Many standards are tin pan alley and Broadway songs from the 30s, 40s and 50s. Others are strictly Jazz compositions. A professional Jazz musician is expected to know many, many standards.

standard tuning - For acoustic and electric guitar, the standard tuning is "E,A,D,G,B,E" (from lowest string to highest). For the electric bass, the standard tuning is "E,A,D,G". Altered tunings are used to obtain lower notes (e.g. drop D tuning, in which the low E string is lowered to a D), facilitate the playing of slide guitar, or to allow the playing of "open" chords that are not possible in standard tuning.

stock arrangement - A commercially published musical arrangement.

stompbox - A slang term which refers to a small, portable effect unit that has an integrated on-off footswitch (e.g. a distortion pedal).

stop-time - A rhythmic device in which the accompanying instruments play a few notes of the rhythm with especially sharp accents, exaggerating the rhythm which, despite its name, does not stop. The "Charleston" rhythm is the most famous of stop-time figures.

Storyville - The New Orleans tenderloin district in which some of the first jazz musicians played. (Storyville was closed in 1917 by the Secretary of the Navy.)...

straight - A more accurate or "legitimate" manner of playing which sticks close to the original music; a notably "square" way of playing.

straight eights - Eighth notes played evenly.

stretch out - An opportunity to play as long as one wishes to.

stride - The typical piano style of the 30s, tending towards virtuosity. The left hand plays alternating low-register bass notes (or octaves, fifths or tenths) and middle register rootless voicings, giving an 'oom-pah' effect, interspersed with step-wise parallel tenths. The right hand often employs busy runs, arpeggios and octaves or full chords. Suggestions of stride remain in the technique of many of today's players.

stroll - A pianist strolls when he or she lays out and allows the rest of the rhythm section to be heard.

substitution - A chord put in the place of a different chord. A substitution can be made throughout a tune, or just ad lib at a particular moment. Usually the operative idea is that the root of the chord is changed, while the other voices are common to both chords. Typical examples bII7 for V7, and iii for I.

subwoofer (sub) - A speaker cabinet with a woofer that is designed for the reproduction of low-frequency sounds from about 20 Hz-200 Hz. Subs are used in PA systems and studio monitor systems. Subwoofers used for PA systems typically use large diameter woofers (18" or 21") mounted in large wooden cabinets. Studio monitor subs tend to use smaller cabinets and smaller-diameter woofers (10", 12", or 15"), because the goal with studio monitors is high fidelity, not massive sound pressure output.

sugar band - A sweet band; lots of vibrato and glissando.

sweet band - A group that plays music that avoids jazz style (swing era) and plays it straight.

sweet spot - In live sound or recordings in which a mic is placed in front of an instrument or a guitar amplifier, the "sweet spot" is a placement or position of a microphone which yields the most pleasing sound; in the context of listening to a mix in a studio through monitor speakers, the "sweet spot" is a distance away from the speakers that the engineer believes to produce the most natural sound.

swing - (1) The style of the 30s, when the big band was the dominant form of Jazz. The style implies certain types of harmony (use of added 6ths rather than 7ths in major and minor chords, of un-embellished diminished chords, frequent use of the augmented 5th and little use of the augmented 11th, etc.) and a rhythmic organization that states the beat explicitly, puts more weight on 1 and 3 and tends to obey the bar-line phrasing. (2) A rhythmic manner, unique to Jazz, in which the first of a pair of written 8th notes is played longer than the second, even twice as long, while the second tends to receive a slight accent, though the distribution of accents is irregular and syncopated. (The degree of this effect depends on the overall tempo, and is modified by the requirements of expression and phrasing.) (3) As a direction in a chart, played with a swing feel, as opposed to latin. (4) A mysterious, unexplainable quality in any music, but especially Jazz, which makes one 'feel that shit all up in your body' (Miles Davis).

swing eighth notes - See swing.

syncopation - The process of displacing 'expected' beats by anticipation or delay of one-half a beat. The natural melodic accent which would fall, in 'square' music, on the beat, is thus heard on the off-beat. This adds a flavor of ambiguity as to where the beat is (not an actual ambiguity, only a flavor).

T

tabulature (tab) - For guitar, bass guitar, and other fretted stringed instruments, tab is a type of sheet music notation in which the strings of the instrument are depicted on paper using staff paper-like lines, and then the pitches to be played are indicated using a fret number on the appropriate string line.

tailgate - A style of trombone playing in early jazz that emphasized bass notes and the ability to play portamentos or "slurs."

take five - A way of telling someone to take a five minute break or to take a five minute break.Hey, Cleanhead, this is a cool tune and we're blowin' too hot. We oughta "take five."

talk - To "tell a story" or "say something" on an instrument: speech-inflected instrumental playing.

tango - An Argentine dance form and music with roots in the 19th century that spread across the world in the early 20th century and now exists in various forms and styles.

tape loop - A loop of recording tape that repeats a sound or sequence of sounds.

technique - the ability of instrumental and vocal musicians to exert optimal control of their instruments or vocal cords in order to produce the precise musical effects they desire. Improving one's technique generally entails practicing exercises that improve one's muscular sensitivity and agility.

tempo - The speed at which a piece of music is moving.

tenor - The voice above the bass, often that played by the thumb of the left hand. Not a Jazz term.

tetrachord - A four-note portion of a scale. For example, the diminished scale is composed of two tetrachords with identical interval constructions.

texture - Musical texture can be thin (a single melody line or a single drum part), thick (two or more layered parts), or very thick (many different types of instruments layered on top of each other, such as the entire Duke Ellington band playing four or five different parts at the same time).

third stream jazz - A form of music that uses both jazz and classical techniques and forms (especially in the late-1950s).

thumb line - The Jazz term for 'tenor' (q.v.). A line played by the pianist's left thumb.

timbre - [pronounced tamb'r] Tone quality, characteristic instrumental sound. Not especially a Jazz term, but note that timbre is one of the basic dimensions of music along with rhythm, melody and harmony. Students sometimes have trouble developing a real Jazz timbre. For the piano the word 'touch' is more usual.

time - A general term for meter, but also the way in which drummers play meter.

time feel - (1) The subjective impression of which time unit constitutes one beat and how long a bar is. May or may not correspond to the written music. (2) The emotional quality of the rhythm.

time/time signature - the number of beats in a *measure*, with one beat being played more strongly than the others; marches or New Orleans jazz are in 2/4 (one-two,one-two), waltzes are in ¾ (one-two-three, one-two-three), most jazz and rock music is in 4/4 (one-two-three-four, one-two-three-four)

tipico - "Typical," "traditional," or "characteristic": a term used to identify popular forms of music with roots in the past of a number of Latin countries and regions.

tonality - Chords and their relationships; the organization of music around a single tone, the tonic.

tone - A single sound, its pitch, volume, timbre, and duration.

tone cluster - Three or more adjacent tones sounded simultaneously.

tonic - The key note of a musical piece; the first note of a scale.

tonic minor - A scale / chord with a minor 3rd and a major 6th and 7th, generally used for the tonic or home chord in minor keys. Distinguished from other minor chord functions.

too much - Just one more jazz superlative. Originally something so good, that it is hard to take. Art Blakey is a fantastic drummer. His playing is "too much."

top - The starting point of a chorus or a piece of music.

trad - (Traditional) the Jazz style of the of the early 1900s, known retrospectively as Dixieland. Used a marked 4/4 beat, triadic harmony, 'sectional' tunes (with numerous separate sections), simultaneous improvisation, largely I - IV - V type harmonies, etc.

trading eights (or 4s, 2s) - A form of discontinuous drum solo in which 4 measure sections are alternately played solo by the drummer, and by the band with another soloist (who goes first). The latter can be one particular soloist throughout, or it can cycle through the different instruments. Also, two different instrumental soloists can trade 4s with each other, such as the trumpet and the sax. This is called a chase. Trading 4s usually goes on for one or two choruses.

train wreck - Event during the playing of a tune when the musicians "disagree" on where they are in the form (i.e. someone gets lost), so the chord changes and the melody may get confused for several bars, but depending on the abilities of the musicians (it happens to the best of them), there are usually no fatalities and the journey continues.

transcription - An arrangement of a piece of music for an instrument or voice for which it was not originally intended.

transpose - To write or perform (a composition) in a key other than the original or given key, most often to accomodate the range of a vocalist or another instrument.

triad - (1) Concretely, a chord of three notes - the root, 3rd and 5th - played together in close position in one of the three inversions. (2) Abstractly, a chord with a root, 3rd and 5th but no 7th. Might be decorated with the 6th or 9th. Triadic harmony is characteristic of Dixieland and rock.

trill - the rapid and repeated alternation of two notes, in the style of many birdsongs

tritone - The interval of three whole steps, i.e. an augmented 4th or diminished 5th.

tritone substitution - See 'Substitution'. The substitution of a chord whose root is a tritone away. In turnarounds it's common to do this for any of the chords.

tubs - Set of drums. Jo is really hot tonight. Listen to him pound those "tubs."

tumbao - A repeated bass or left-hand piano pattern; various patterns usually played by the bongos. Along with the clave, the tumbao forms the basis of Cuban-derived music.

tune: A single Jazz composition or Jazz performance, a piece. The word 'song' is frowned on.

turnaround - A sequence of chords, or the portion of a tune that they occupy, that forms a cadence at the end of a section of a tune, definitively establishes the tonic key and leads back to the opening chord of the next section, or to the top. Typically the turnaround chords are I - VI - ii - V, with half a measure apiece. With possible substitutions and alterations, the variations are infinite. There are also entirely different progressions possible. If the opening chord of the next section is not a I chord, the turnaround must be suitable. Learning to negotiate turnarounds is essential to making a coherent solo. It's often effective to play a phrase that starts partway through a turnaround and continues past the beginning of the next section.

turning the beat around - Also "turning the rhythm section around." To lose the beat, either by mistake, or to briefly heighten tension before returning to the beat.

two-beat - Also "playing in two." A form of rhythm organization in which the first and third beats of the bar are emphasized (particularly by the bass), often leaving the second and fourth beats silent, with a resulting "boom-chick" feel. Two-beat was...

U

up tempo - The fastest of the jazz tempos.

up-beat - One or more notes at the beginning of a melody that begin before the first bar line.

upper structure - A triad used in the upper register over a chord of a different root, such as an A major triad over a C7 chord. From the standpoint of C7, the A triad consists of the 13th, the flat 9th, and the 3rd; at the same time it has the unified sound of a major triad.

V

vamp - A simple section like a riff, designed to be repeated as often as necessary, especially one at the beginning of a tune. Also a constantly repeated bass line over which a solo is played.

verse - In many older standard songs, an introductory section, often rubato, that leads up to the 'chorus' or main strain, which is the tune as generally recognized. Jazz players (and fakebooks) usually omit the verse, though singers like to use them.

vibrato - The rapid pulsing or wavering of a tone.

vocalese - Words set to a recorded instrumental solo improvisation.

voice - Any one of the melodic lines formed by the flow of the music. The bass line and the melody form the two outer voices, and the tones in between may, to a greater or lesser extent, form melodic lines of their own called inner voices.

voice-leading - Getting the succession of harmonic tones in the inner voices to form coherent melodic lines of their own, or, at least, to move in a smooth, mainly step-wise motion. The perfection of voice-leading was in Bach, where 4 or more independent melodies can mesh to form perfect chordal harmony.

voicing - The placement of notes in a chord; the instruments that are assigned to those notes.

W

wah wah mute/pedal - A mute used to create a laughing or talking sound on a brass instrument; a device that creates those sounds on amplified instruments such as the guitar or the electric piano...

wail - To play a tune extremely well. Count Basie did a tune called "Prince of Wails" -- a clever play on words. Damn, Basie's band can really "wail."

walk - Also "walking." In bass playing, to play mostly one note per beat, making a smooth, continuous quarter-note line. A fulfillment of the time-keeping function of bass playing, which many bass players have transcended since around 1960. The pianist can also walk with his left hand.

walking bass or walking rhythm - an energetic four-beat rhythm pattern. I really dig the way Earl plays the 88's. He plays the tune with his left hand and a "walking bass" with his right.

waltz - a song in ¾ time (see *time/time signature*)

West Coast jazz - A much criticized label for the 'Cool' style (q.v.) as it was taken up in California in the early 50s by mostly white players, like Dave Brubeck, Gerry Mulligan, Chet Baker and many lesser figures like pianist Russ Freeman. In addition to the typical features of cool Jazz, the style experimented with 'classical' instruments and complex counterpoint.

whole tone - A 6-note scale, of which there are two, made up entirely of whole-step intervals, or the harmonies derived from it.

wig, **Wig out** - To flip out. Also to think precisely.I don't know what happened, man, we were just sittin' there and Louie just "wigged out."

wild - Astonishing or amazing.It's really "wild" the way Lee plays the trumpet.

witch Doctor - A member of the clergy.Have you heard, Margie's brother is a "witch doctor."

woodshed - [also know as: shedding] To practice diligently. Also 'shed'.

X

X - 'Time'. Thus ' 4X ' on a chart means '[play] four times'

Y

young lions - a sub-genre of jazz also known as *neo-bop* (see the entry for *neo-bop*under Schools of Jazz at the end of this glossary)

Z

zoot - (obsolete) Used in the thirties and forties to describe exaggerated clothes, especially a zoot suit. Look at that cat's "zoot" suit. It's crazy, man.

zozzled - drunk